THE CHINESE HOROSCOPES LIBRARY

Ox

KWOK MAN-HO

DORLING KINDERSLEY
LONDON • NEW YORK • STUTTGART

A DORLING KINDERSLEY BOOK

Senior Editor Sharon Lucas
Art Editor Camilla Fox
Managing Editor Krystyna Mayer
Managing Art Editor Derek Coombes
DTP Designer Doug Miller
Production Controller Antony Heller

Artworks: Danuta Mayer 4, 8, 11, 17, 27, 29, 31, 33, 35;
Giuliano Fornari 21; Studio Illibill 25; Jane Thomson; Sarah Ponder.

Special Photography by Steve Gorton. Thank you to The British Museum, Chinese Post
Office, Percival David Foundation of Chinese Art, and The Powell-Cotton Museum.

Additional Photography: Eric Crichton, Jo Foord, Steve Gorton, Dave King, David Murray,
Stephen Oliver, Tim Ridley, Clive Streeter, Matthew Ward.

Picture Credits: Bridgeman Art Library/Oriental Museum, Durham University 12; Courtesy
of The Board of Trustees of the Victoria & Albert Museum 15.

First published in Great Britain in 1994
by Dorling Kindersley Limited,
9 Henrietta Street, London WC2E 8PS

Copyright © 1994 Dorling Kindersley Limited, London
Text copyright © 1994 ICOREC

A CIP catalogue record for this book is available from the British Library

ISBN 0-7513-0117-5

Reproduced by GRB Editrice, Verona, Italy
Printed and bound in Hong Kong by Imago

CONTENTS

INTRODUCING CHINESE HOROSCOPES

For thousands of years, the Chinese have used their astrology and religion to establish a harmony between people and the world around them.

The exact origins of the twelve animals of Chinese astrology – the Rat, Ox, Tiger, Rabbit, Dragon, Snake, Horse, Ram, Monkey, Rooster, Dog, and Pig – remain a mystery. Nevertheless, these animals are important in Chinese astrology. They are much more than general signposts to the year, and to the possible good or bad times ahead for us all. The twelve animals of Chinese astrology are considered to be a reflection of the Universe itself.

YIN AND YANG SYMBOL
White represents the female force of yin, and black represents the masculine force of yang.

every single thing in the Universe is held in balance by the dynamic, cosmic forces of yin and yang. Yin is feminine, watery, and cool; the force of the Moon and the rain. Yang is masculine, solid, and hot; the force of the Sun and the Earth. According to ancient Chinese belief, the concentrated essences of yin and yang became the four seasons, and the scattered essences of yin and yang became the myriad creatures that are found on Earth.

The twelve animals of Chinese astrology are all associated with either yin or yang. The forces of yin rise as winter approaches. These forces decline with the warmth of spring, when yang begins to assert

YIN AND YANG

The many differences in our natures, moods, health, and fortunes reflect the wider changes within the Universe. The Chinese believe that itself. Even in the course of a normal day, yin and yang are at work, constantly changing and balancing. These forces also naturally rise and fall within us all.

Everyone has their own internal balance of yin and yang. This affects our tempers, ambitions, and health. We also respond to the changes of weather, to the environment, and to the people who surround us.

THE FIVE ELEMENTS

All that we can touch, taste, or see is divided into five basic types or elements – wood, fire, earth, gold, and water. Everything in the Universe can be linked to one of these elements.

For example, the element earth is linked to four animals – the Ox, Dragon, Ram, and Dog. This element is also linked to the colour yellow, sweet-tasting food, and the emotion of desire. The activity of these various elements indicates the fortune that may befall us.

AN INDIVIDUAL DISCOVERY

Chinese astrology can help you balance your yin and yang. It can also tell you which element you are, and the colours, tastes, parts of the body, or emotions that are linked to your particular sign. Your fortune can be prophesied according to the year, month, day, and hour in which you were born. You can identify the type of people to whom you are attracted, and the career that will suit your character. You can understand your changes of mood, your reactions to other places, and to other people. In essence, you can start to discover what makes you an individual.

DIVINATION STICKS
Another ancient and popular method of Chinese fortune-telling is using special divination sticks to obtain a specific reading from prediction books.

CASTING YOUR HOROSCOPE

*The Chinese calendar is based on the movement of the
Moon, unlike the calendar used in the Western world,
which is based on the movement of the Sun.*

Before you begin to cast your
Chinese horoscope, check your year
of birth on the chart on pages 44 to
45. Check particularly carefully if
you were born in the early months of
the year. The Chinese year does not
usually begin until January or
February, and you might belong to the
previous Chinese year. For
example, if you were born in 1961
you might assume that you were
born in the Year of the Ox.
However, if your birthday falls
before 15 February you belong to the
previous Chinese year, which is the
Year of the Rat.

THE SIXTY-YEAR CYCLE

The Chinese measure the passing of
time by cycles of sixty years. The
twelve astrological animals appear
five times during the sixty-year
cycle, and they appear in a slightly
different form every time. For
example, if you were born in 1949

you are an Ox Inside the Gate, but if
you were born in 1961, you are an
Ox on the Way.

MONTHS, DAYS, AND HOURS

The twelve lunar months of the
Chinese calendar do not correspond
exactly with the twelve Western
calendar months. This is because
Chinese months are lunar, whereas
Western months are solar. Chinese
months are normally twenty-nine to
thirty days long, and every three to
four years an extra month is added to
keep approximately in step with the
Western year.

One Chinese hour is equal to two
Western hours, and the twelve
Chinese hours correspond to the
twelve animal signs.

The year, month, day, and hour
of birth are the keys to Chinese
astrology. Once you know them,
you can start to unlock your personal
Chinese horoscope.

	Water	
	Earth	Gold
	Wood	Yin
	Fire	Yang

CHINESE ASTROLOGICAL WHEEL
In the centre of the wheel is the yin and yang symbol. It is surrounded by the Chinese astrological character linked to each animal. The band of colour reveals your element, and the outer ring shows whether you are yin or yang.

· OX ·
MYTHS AND LEGENDS

According to Chinese legend, the Jade Emperor, the ruler of Heaven, asked to see the Earth's twelve most interesting animals, then awarded the Ox second place.

The ox is a highly respected creature because it ploughs the land and helps with the harvest. Many Chinese do not eat beef, considering it unjust to kill the creature that deserves thanks. The ox is a symbol of spring, traditionally the time of the ceremonial ploughing. It is also linked to water, and bronze or stone figures of oxen were often thrown into rivers in the belief that they would stop the riverbanks from bursting.

FARMER CHIN AND THE OX

Long ago, Farmer Chin had a very small field of hard soil in which nothing had grown for years. He bought an ox, a big, gentle

GLASS SNUFF BOTTLE
This Chinese, 18th-century, glass snuff bottle depicts an old man astride an ox.

creature. Seeing the poverty of Farmer Chin's family, the good, kind ox was determined to do all he could to help. The ox and the farmer worked from dawn to dusk. The ox's power and strength broke the soil, and his manure was used as fertilizer for the young plants. Fifteen years later, the farmer was wealthy, and had a large house full of servants. But the old ox still lived in his little pen, ate poor food, and had to work very hard. One day, the ox broke a leg. "What use is that ox to me?" said Farmer Chin, and ordered that it be slaughtered. An old man suddenly approached, and said, "This ox has helped you make

12

your fortune. Can't you now allow him to rest?" Farmer Chin ignored the old man. As the ox's throat was cut, Farmer Chin felt a terrible pain in his neck. He fell to the ground, dead, and the ox and the old man disappeared in an instant.

The farmer's soul was grasped and dragged into a courtroom. It contained the old man, who was King Ch'in-kuang, ruler of the first Hell. Beside him stood the old ox, now transformed into an official of the court of Hell.

The ox took Farmer Chin to a mirror. "Look within," boomed the king. "See all the creatures whose lives you have taken for food or sport." All the animals and birds the farmer had ever eaten or killed appeared in the mirror, including the old ox. The king ordered that Farmer Chin be thrown into the most terrible pit for his lack of compassion for all creatures, but most especially, for the kind ox.

Chinese legend still says that the first official to be seen after death is the ox-headed god of the first Hell.

OX-HEADED TOMB FIGURE
The exact date of this Chinese, ox-headed tomb figure is unknown, and it may even be fairly modern. It is made of gilded bronze.

· OX ·
PERSONALITY

Honest, placid, and always considerate, the Ox never acts on mere whim. It refuses to be influenced by gossip or trivia, and ponders all the angles of every situation.

Once you have completed a thorough assessment of any situation, you carry your course of action through to the appropriate end. You need plenty of time to build up your considerable reserves of strength. Although you may be slow to start, by the time others are exhausted or confused, you can still be found in steady pursuit of your goal.

MOTIVATION
You are very sure of your own mind, and will not be swayed. If your interest is not aroused, no amount of temptation and persuasion will make you respond or react. You are solidly reliable, and always mean and do

what you say. You have a strong streak of stubbornness, and a tendency to be outspoken. These traits often make you resistant to advice, and you can be intolerant and scathing towards people who do not share your persistence.

THE INNER OX
Essentially, you are stable and well balanced, and your steadiness is a genuine inspiration to other people. However, if you are provoked, or if your patience is pushed to its limits, your temper is furious and unrelenting.

At these times it is best for you to be left alone, since you can only calm down of your own accord. You are

MEDALLION BOWL
This Ch'ing dynasty, yellow-ground medallion bowl depicts the Ox in a late winter scene.

CLOISONNE OX
*Sturdy and upright,
this Chinese, ox-shaped
vessel suggests the strength,
stature, and stubbornness of the
Ox personality. It is cloisonné
enamel on copper with gilding,
and dates from the Ch'ing
dynasty (1749–1795).*

an independent character, and are not easily impressed by the fashionable. You are much more comfortable and secure with the traditional and the familiar.

You dislike any form of change, particularly if it is forced upon you. However, you are invariably able to cope with most situations.

If you do have any doubts about yourself and the direction in which you are heading, you much prefer to keep your own counsel.

You are a faithful and trustworthy friend, and will always be helpful in times of need.

In emotional affairs, you are not particularly passionate or romantic, but you are faithful and caring.

THE OX CHILD
The young Ox is serious and practical, but may be too dedicated to its schoolwork. It needs every encouragement to relax, have fun, and enjoy itself.

· OX ·
LOVE

Steadiness, reliability, and sincerity are much more important to the Ox than tumultuous emotion, searing passion, or the trappings of romance.

Once you have found your partner, you are likely to be thoroughly devoted and loving. You need to be absolutely sure of your own mind before you commit yourself to anyone, but once you have made a commitment, you remain sincere. Your partner should never make the mistake of taking advantage of you, for once you have been deceived, you are unlikely ever to forgive or forget.

You may neglect romantic anniversaries, but you will always be available when your loved one needs support. Occasionally, a stubborn streak may rise to the surface, but nevertheless, you try not to be hurtful.

Ideally, you are suited to the Rooster or the Snake. The sociable Rooster acts as a complement to your steady nature, and you are equally reasonable and reliable. The Snake will feel safe and secure in your presence, and will happily allow you to arrange its home life. You should find the Rat's intelligence and sincerity highly attractive, and the Rat will enjoy

GODDESS OF LOVE
Kuan Yin is a powerful figure in Chinese mythology. Once a male Buddhist deity, she is now known as the goddess of mercy, and as Sung-tzu, the giver of children.

CHINESE COMPATIBILITY WHEEL

Find your animal sign, then look for the animals that share its background colour – the Ox has a yellow background, and is most compatible with the Snake and the Rooster. The symbol in the centre of the wheel represents double happiness.

your earnestness. The mischievous Monkey is a particularly good match for you – it appreciates your honesty, and will gently tease you when you become too serious. Your steady nature appeals to the Rabbit, who always needs to feel harmonious and secure. The Pig will welcome your fondness for peace and quiet, although it is likely to find your innate good sense rather frustrating at times.

ORCHID
In China, the orchid, or Lan Hua, *is an emblem of love and beauty. It is also a fertility symbol, and represents many offspring.*

Unfortunately, your romantic forecast is not quite so healthy when considering emotional relationships with the Ram, Horse, Dragon, or Dog. This is mainly because the Ram thinks and acts too quickly, the Horse is too lively and passionate, and the Dragon and the Dog are too wilful and imaginative.

The Tiger is also unlikely to be a good partner for you – its sheer unpredictability will disturb you, and your conscientiousness will not suit the Tiger's wandering spirit.

· OX ·
CAREER

The Ox is a thorough and efficient worker. It does not take kindly to interruption or interference, but will gladly take on the burden of responsibility.

Wheat

FARMER
Harvesting crops, collecting dairy produce, and working on the land are satisfying pursuits for the extremely hardworking Ox.

Dairy produce

Chinese rouge box

OX ON A BOX
This rouge box is from 17th- or early 18th-century China. The Chinese consider the Ox to be a beast of burden, and here it is depicted carrying an old man, probably Lao Tzu, the legendary founder of Taoism.

Chinese musical instrument

ESTATE MANAGER
The position of estate manager requires fine attention to detail, and a willingness to take responsibility. The Ox possesses both of these qualities, and has the added bonus of a steady, reliable personality. The natural attribute of thinking carefully before making important decisions is useful to an estate manager.

Estate manager's keys

Oven glove

WORKER WITH FOOD
In China, the Ox is known as the beast that draws the plough. As a result, the Ox is well suited to working with agricultural products.

TEACHER
The Ox makes an excellent teacher, for it relishes a busy and well-organized schedule. Perhaps a teacher taught a pupil to play this bronze musical instrument in China in the 1st century BC.

Soldier's boots

ARMED FORCES
If the Ox decides to join the armed forces, it is likely to be extremely successful. It is singleminded, and will not regret its decision.

· OX ·
HEALTH

Yin and yang are in a continual state of flux within the body. Good health is dependent upon the balance of yin and yang being constantly harmonious.

There is a natural minimum and maximum level of yin and yang in the human body. The body's energy is known as ch'i, and is a yang force. The movement of ch'i in the human body is complemented by the movement of blood, which is a yin force. The very slightest displacement of the balance of yin or yang in the human body can quickly lead to poor health and sickness.

LINGCHIH FUNGUS
The fungus shown in this detail from a Ch'ing dynasty bowl is the "immortal" lingchih fungus, which symbolizes longevity.

GINGER ROOT
In Chinese medicine, ginger root is usually prescribed for its abundant yang, or warming, qualities.

However, yang illness can be cured by yin treatment, and yin illness can be cured by yang treatment. Everybody has their own individual balance of yin and yang. It is likely that a hot-tempered person will have strong yang forces, and that a peaceful person will have strong yin forces. Your nature is closely identified with your health, and before Chinese medicine can be prescribed, your moods must be carefully taken into account. A balance of joy, anger, sadness, happiness, worry, pensiveness, and fear must always be maintained. This fine balance is known in China as the Harmony of the Seven Sentiments.

Born in the Year of the Ox, you are associated with the element earth. This element is linked with the spleen, pancreas, stomach, muscles, and mouth. These are the parts of the human body that are most relevant to the pattern of your health. You are also associated with the emotion of desire, and with sweet-tasting food.

Ginger root (*Zingiber officinale*) is associated with your astrological sign. It is used for its yang, or warming qualities, which can combat symptoms of nausea, dissipate phlegm, and stimulate the stomach and the intestines.

Ginger root can be prescribed as treatment for colds, or for any ailments that involve coughing. Preserved ginger root is often used to alleviate motion sickness.

Chinese medicine is highly specific, therefore never take ginger root or any other natural medicine unless you are following advice from a Chinese or Western doctor.

ASTROLOGY AND ANATOMY

Your element, earth, is associated with the digestive system. The stomach is a yang organ, and the pancreas, found behind the stomach, is a yin organ.

· OX ·
LEISURE

The Ox has a placid, but determined, nature. It has excellent reserves of physical energy, and once it has taken up a new activity, it pursues it wholeheartedly.

BOXING AND WRESTLING
The Ox is immensely strong and energetic, but it is not particularly aggressive. Boxing and wrestling are ideal sports for the Ox, because they allow it to use its strength and expend its energy in a skilful way within a controlled environment.

Boxing gloves

Camelskin rugby ball

High-sided rugby boot

RUGBY
Playing rugby has great appeal for the Ox – it is a traditional sport, and the Ox is rarely interested in or impressed by the latest fads or fashions. Rugby was first played in 1823 at Rugby school in England, hence the sport's name. It is also a very physical sport, in which the Ox can use its strength and endurance, while enjoying being outdoors among the elements.

WINING AND DINING

Hospitality is one of the Ox's best qualities. It is happiest in the company of old friends, and is most comfortable in a familiar environment. Consequently, it loves to wine and dine at home, and will make every effort to ensure the comfort of its guests.

Glasses of wine and red rose

Ski

OX VASE

This aubergine and turquoise ox was used as a vase in Ch'ing dynasty China (1662–1722).

Salopettes and gloves

Porcelain ox

SKIING

The Ox finds skiing exhilarating because it is a very physical outdoor sport. The Ox also enjoys being outside in a hard, cold environment, and likes to keep its powerful body under control – skiing allows it to do so.

· OX ·
SYMBOLISM

In Chinese astrology, each of the twelve animals is linked with a certain food, direction, colour, emotion, association, and symbol.

Chinese ox

COLOUR
In China, fertile earth has a yellow hue. Yellow was the imperial colour, worn by the emperor as the First Son of the Earth. The colour yellow is also linked with the Ox. This yellow gold, glazed model of an ox is from China's Ch'ing dynasty.

FOOD
There are five tastes according to Chinese astrology – salty, acrid, bitter, sweet, and sour. Sweet foods, such as cashew nuts, are associated with the Ox.

Cashew nuts

Antique
Chinese
compass

Section of a
map of Rome

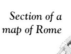

DIRECTION

*The Chinese compass points south, whereas
the Western compass points north. The
Chinese compass has an extra direction,
the centre, which is the Ox's direction.*

ASSOCIATION

*The capital city and its life are
linked with the Ox.*

SYMBOL

*The Ox's symbol is the plumb line, which
is used to measure the depth of water.*

Plumb line

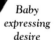

EMOTION

*Desire is the emotion that is
connected with the Ox.*

Baby
expressing
desire

OX IN THE SEA

~ 1925 1985 ~

According to Chinese legend, the Ox led the race to cross the
waters to be the first animal in the Chinese calendar, but
was robbed of victory by the Rat.

Water is a safe and comfortable environment for any Ox, and the Ox in the Sea is particularly strong and tenacious. It is likely that you have always lived happily and confidently in your environment.

CHILDHOOD
When you were a child, there were probably many people to care for you, such as your parents, other relatives, and friends. Their love and encouragement gave you an extremely positive start in life.

PERSONALITY
You are linked to a seedling leaving the seed and reaching towards the light. In the same way that the seedling blossoms when it eventually reaches the light, so you have been guided throughout your life to realize your full potential. You are also associated with spring, a time

renowned for growth and new life. This means that you are blessed by powerful forces.

You are a good learner, and are willing to tackle anything new, even though this goes against the grain of the usually reticent Ox.

FEMALE CHARACTERISTICS
The female Ox in the Sea is highly talented, but may sometimes need to watch her temper. She is invariably self-assured, but could be more patient with those who do not share her sense of security.

RELATIONSHIPS
Oxen in the Sea should find little difficulty in attracting other people, and will usually have happy and successful relationships. However, you have a desire to travel and to enjoy the stimulus of new places, faces, and challenges.

Ox in the Sea

PARENTHOOD

It should be possible for you to develop a rewarding relationship with your children. This relationship holds great personal importance for you. It is always worth considerable nurture, particularly as your own relationship with your parents could prove unsatisfactory over the years.

As you grow older, and become more confident, it is likely that you will simply have to be independent and go your own way in life. Your family may sometimes find this difficult to understand, but you should be able to dispel any tension by always being willing to rebuild the bridges between you.

OX IN THE LAKE

~ 1937 1997 ~

In China, water buffalo calmly stand their ground in the paddy fields, robust and unswerving. The Ox in the Lake is equally sturdy and self-confident in any environment.

You are associated with a nail, which symbolizes steadfastness and solidity. The nail is the pivot, and it also holds all things together. You are invariably extremely stable throughout your life – you stand firm while everything swirls around you like the waters of a lake.

PERSONALITY
You are secure, calm, and kind. Because you are perceived to be very dependable, many people should feel that they can confide in you.

All Oxen in the Lake tend to be competent and skilled, but the female in particular is noted for her abilities, and for the way in which she uses her talents to the full.

CAREER
Your career is highly likely to be prosperous because you are a person of your word and can always be

depended upon when times become difficult. As long as you remain true to your calling, your reliability is likely to bring you happiness and financial security.

However, do not expect wealth to come too quickly, and remember that it is highly unlikely to be made overnight at someone else's expense. Instead, your fortune will be accrued gradually, as a result of years of hard, honest work, and as people learn to put their trust in you.

RELATIONSHIPS
If you are careful in your choice of partner, you can have a good relationship. Since you are so dependable, you have the ability to help the flighty to settle, and can also act as a rock for the weak.

You must always beware of unscrupulous characters such as the Rat, however, who will attempt to

Ox in the Lake

prey upon your charity, rely upon your strength, and use you for their own ends – try not to allow your good nature to be exploited.

Because you never rush into things, you are likely to have children in your later years. This will probably be for the best, because you will have become more capable of supplying your children with the necessary love, support, and care.

PROSPECTS

Do not expect too much of your youth, since it is during these early years that you will develop most of your strengths. Instead, try to look forward to your middle years, when you are much more likely to reap what you have sown.

The trust people have placed in you over the years should be rewarded, and you will have become known as a trustworthy person. People will increasingly turn to you for guidance, and as a result, your own career and fortune are likely to blossom. If you remain true to yourself, you should end your days respected and at peace.

OX INSIDE THE GATE

~ 1949 2009 ~

The Ox Inside the Gate tends to be an impatient creature. It wants to enjoy its freedom, and consequently finds any restriction to be extremely unpleasant.

You are linked to the warp and the weft of thread which is woven together. This signifies that you are meant to be part of a larger whole, but there is always likely to be part of you that wants to break free.

PERSONALITY

Your impatience and curtness are often likely to make you speak your mind openly. Try to take care that your love of forthright speaking and of telling the plain truth are not unnecessarily cutting and hurtful to other people.

Your abruptness is usually admirable if you know how to use such insight wisely, but it can be damaging and painful if used indiscriminately, or just for effect.

It will do you no harm to remember that although you are an Ox Inside the Gate, and wish to push it aside carelessly and rush off to

enjoy your liberty, nevertheless a significant part of you is also called to be part of the weft and warp of a much greater pattern.

All Oxen are likely to be strong and dependable, and you will always find yourself in demand. This can be unsettling for you, because you have a tendency to go against the grain.

Try to control the rebellious habit of going off and doing what you want. It is likely that money will always restrain you, anyway. Do not fight against this – instead try to see it as a useful constraint.

FEMALE CHARACTERISTICS

Because of the influence of the yin force, the Female Ox Inside the Gate is renowned for being clever, and for involving herself in all kinds of issues. She invariably resents the barriers that restrain her, and will gladly lead the fight for equal rights.

Ox Inside the Gate

However, she may have to watch this confrontational tendency, and should discern between the barriers that matter and those that do not.

RELATIONSHIPS

Anyone born in these years is likely to be very attractive, both physically and mentally. Consequently, you may find yourself the centre of considerable attention. Combined with your wish to break free from anything that restricts you, this could mean that you will have more than one committed relationship.

Sometimes your relationship may seem like the Gate that confines you. Always make sure that it is absolutely necessary for you to break free, and carefully consider whether you can remain woven into the fabric of this relationship. Try not to act hastily, but do not be too surprised when you do, for it is in your nature to behave in this way.

By the time you reach your late middle age, you should feel more content, and your career and personal relationships are likely to blossom around this time.

OX ON THE WAY

~ 1901 1961 ~

Your own way in life can sometimes seem unclear, but your Ox perseverance and strength should help you to meet the challenges that you will invariably face.

You are highly sociable, enjoyable company, and have a friendly nature. Others think very highly of you, and you are always willing to put yourself out for them. You have good, rewarding friendships, too. A certain sadness is linked with you, however, and if it is not handled correctly, it can soon turn to bitterness.

YOUTH

When you were in your youth, it is likely that something frightening happened to you. It could have been an accident, a disappointment, an unpleasant experience, or even an upsetting failure at something that you considered important. Whatever it may have been, you run the risk of being knocked off course for life.

You need to learn to live with whatever has happened in your past. Try not to allow it to make you cynical or resentful, for this could

spoil your basically good nature. Once you have explored these negative feelings and have them under control, you should find that your life is very much easier to live and to enjoy.

FEMALE CHARACTERISTICS

The female Ox on the Way should never despair, for she has a very good chance of leading a happy and comfortable life. As long as she learns to cope with any early disappointments in a positive way, and if she is blessed with a little luck, she should easily fulfil her potential.

CAREER

The professional life of any Ox on the Way is unlikely to be overly problematic, and your skills should be in high demand. Unfortunately, this does not necessarily mean that you will be wealthy.

Ox on the Way

As with all Oxen, wealth will only come to you through hard work and over a long period of time. Do not rush, nor expect too much too soon. Because you are associated with the autumn, you should find prosperity and peace in your later years.

RELATIONSHIPS

Any Ox born in these years is likely to have happy relationships and a good family life, but could also experience some difficult times.

Problems of an emotional nature can be avoided if you try not to make hasty decisions concerning your family, and if you do not expect too much help from them. Look instead to your considerable inner strengths and to the many good friends who truly appreciate you.

PROSPECTS

The passing of time and a little patience should ensure that you end your days in a happy and contented state. By taking careful stock of yourself, you can reasonably expect a long, contented life. But do not be in a hurry – wealth and security are likely to be a gift of time, and of your own strength of resolve.

OX OUTSIDE THE GATE

~ 1913 1973 ~

This is an immensely powerful Ox. For the Ox Outside the Gate, the innate strength of the Ox is combined with the blessing brought about by correct behaviour.

You are associated with winter. This is a symbol of old age and death, but the Ox Outside the Gate is also associated with happy, auspicious days. This means that if you always do the right thing, you will enjoy good fortune, and even the dead days of winter should be enlivened.

You are linked with a grass mat, on which offerings to the dead were placed. This symbolism is highly propitious, for any offerings made to the dead should ensure that the living gain great benefit and merit.

PERSONALITY

You tend to want to do things properly, and are usually rewarded. You should have a successful life, and earn great respect, but do not be surprised if it takes some time before you achieve your rewards. Try not to lose heart when life does not go your way immediately.

FEMALE CHARACTERISTICS

The female Ox Outside the Gate has a tendency to be unthinking in her actions. She invariably finds it easier to be off-hand when she should be polite, and to be cutting in her remarks when it might be wiser to restrain herself.

She is well-advised to attempt to balance her considerable wit and intellect with politeness and respect for others, and should always be prepared to apologize for any unreasonable behaviour.

CAREER

Try to learn to be patient, for in the early stages of your life and your career, financial benefit and promotion are likely to come slowly.

Your family is probably not wealthy, and is unlikely to be able to offer you financial help. Your powers of persistence should bring their own

Ox Outside the Gate

rewards, however. In the same way, your good behaviour should help you to earn the respect of others, and this is likely to be highly beneficial for your career.

RELATIONSHIPS

All Oxen Outside the Gate are likely to have their serious emotional relationships later in life. When you have found the right partner, your relationship should be good, but try not to have children too quickly. Children may place unnecessary strain upon you when you are young. They will invariably force financial demands upon you, and you will be better equipped to face these challenges once you have begun to progress in your career.

YOUR CHINESE MONTH OF BIRTH

Find the table with your year of birth, and see where your birthday falls. For example, if you were born on 30 August 1949, you were born in Chinese month 7.

1 You are hardworking and successful, but can often appear to be awkward and distant.

2 You are happy and contented, but can occasionally be naive in your assessments of other people.

3 You are singleminded, and prefer to be alone. You loathe criticism, but should try to listen.

4 You are determined to succeed, and will make many sacrifices. Try to develop your compassion.

5 You are tough, and hate to lose. You are also kind, however, and are always willing to join in.

6 You are outwardly confident, but inwardly worried. Learn to live with these personal contradictions.

7 Beware of your tendency to use any means to succeed. Try to listen more, and to act less.

8 You are vivacious, likable, and attractive. Your strong personality should help you succeed in life.

9 You are compassionate, kind, and intelligent. Others like and trust you, but you should always beware of unscrupulous people.

10 You are successful and sociable. Your love life may start unhappily, but should eventually blossom.

11 You love to face a challenge, and are a natural leader. You have a keen sense of justice, which can make you feel combative.

12 You are funny, determined, and a good friend. You might set yourself standards that are too high.

* Some Chinese years contain double months:	
1925: Month 4	1949: Month 7
23 April – 21 May	26 July – 23 Aug
22 May – 20 June	24 Aug – 21 Sept

1901	
19 Feb – 19 March	1
20 March – 18 April	2
19 April – 17 May	3
18 May – 15 June	4
16 June – 15 July	5
16 July – 13 Aug	6
14 Aug – 12 Sept	7
13 Sept – 11 Oct	8
12 Oct – 10 Nov	9
11 Nov – 10 Dec	10
11 Dec – 9 Jan 1902	11
10 Jan – 7 Feb	12

1913	
6 Feb – 7 March	1
8 March – 6 April	2
7 April – 5 May	3
6 May – 4 June	4
5 June – 3 July	5
4 July – 1 Aug	6
2 Aug – 31 Aug	7
1 Sept – 29 Sept	8
30 Sept – 28 Oct	9
29 Oct – 27 Nov	10
28 Nov – 26 Dec	11
27 Dec – 25 Jan 1914	12

1925	
24 Jan – 22 Feb	1
23 Feb – 23 March	2
24 March – 22 April	3
* See double months box	4
21 June – 20 July	5
21 July – 18 Aug	6
19 Aug – 17 Sept	7
18 Sept – 17 Oct	8
18 Oct – 15 Nov	9
16 Nov – 15 Dec	10
16 Dec – 13 Jan 1926	11
14 Jan – 12 Feb	12

1937	
11 Feb – 12 March	1
13 March – 10 April	2
11 April – 9 May	3
10 May – 8 June	4
9 June – 7 July	5
8 July – 5 Aug	6
6 Aug – 4 Sept	7
5 Sept – 3 Oct	8
4 Oct – 2 Nov	9
3 Nov – 2 Dec	10
3 Dec – 1 Jan 1938	11
2 Jan – 30 Jan	12

1949	
29 Jan – 27 Feb	1
28 Feb – 28 March	2
29 March – 27 April	3
28 April – 27 May	4
28 May – 25 June	5
26 June – 25 July	6
* See double months box	7
22 Sept – 21 Oct	8
22 Oct – 19 Nov	9
20 Nov – 19 Dec	10
20 Dec – 17 Jan 1950	11
18 Jan – 16 Feb	12

1961	
15 Feb – 16 March	1
17 March – 14 April	2
15 April – 14 May	3
15 May – 12 June	4
13 June – 12 July	5
13 July – 10 Aug	6
11 Aug – 9 Sept	7
10 Sept – 9 Oct	8
10 Oct – 7 Nov	9
8 Nov – 7 Dec	10
8 Dec – 5 Jan 1962	11
6 Jan – 4 Feb	12

1973	
3 Feb – 4 March	1
5 March – 2 April	2
3 April – 2 May	3
3 May – 31 May	4
1 June – 29 June	5
30 June – 29 July	6
30 July – 27 Aug	7
28 Aug – 25 Sept	8
26 Sept – 25 Oct	9
26 Oct – 24 Nov	10
25 Nov – 23 Dec	11
24 Dec – 22 Jan 1974	12

1985	
20 Feb – 20 March	1
21 March – 19 April	2
20 April – 19 May	3
20 May – 17 June	4
18 June – 17 July	5
18 July – 15 Aug	6
16 Aug – 14 Sept	7
15 Sept – 13 Oct	8
14 Oct – 11 Nov	9
12 Nov – 11 Dec	10
12 Dec – 9 Jan 1986	11
10 Jan – 8 Feb	12

1997	
7 Feb – 8 March	1
9 March – 6 April	2
7 April – 6 May	3
7 May – 4 June	4
5 June – 4 July	5
5 July – 2 Aug	6
3 Aug – 1 Sept	7
2 Sept – 1 Oct	8
2 Oct – 30 Oct	9
31 Oct – 29 Nov	10
30 Nov – 29 Dec	11
30 Dec – 27 Jan 1998	12

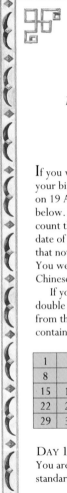

YOUR CHINESE
DAY OF BIRTH

*Refer to the previous page to discover the beginning of your
Chinese month of birth, then use the chart below to
calculate your Chinese day of birth.*

If you were born on 5 May 1901,
your birthday is in the month starting
on 19 April. Find 19 on the chart
below. Using 19 as the first day,
count the days until you reach the
date of your birthday. Remember
that not all months contain 31 days.
You were born on day 17 of the
Chinese month.

If you were born in a Chinese
double month, simply count the days
from the first date of the month that
contains your birthday.

1	2	3	4	5	6	7
8	9	10	11	12	13	14
15	16	17	18	19	20	21
22	23	24	25	26	27	28
29	30	31				

DAY 1, 10, 19, OR 28
You are trustworthy, and set high
standards, but tend to rush your

projects. Try to be cautious, and do
not be too self-obsessed. You may
receive unexpected money, but must
control your spending. You are
suited to a career in the public sector
or the arts.

DAY 2, 11, 20, OR 29
You are honest and popular. You
need peace, but also require lively
company. You are prone to
outbursts of temper. You tend to
enjoy life, and make the most of your
opportunities. You are suited to a
literary or artistic career.

DAY 3, 12, 21, OR 30
You are quick-witted, but may
appear to be difficult. As a result,
people may be wary of being your
friend. You have a disciplined
character, and fight for the truth.
You are suited to careers that have a
competitive element.

DAY 4, 13, 22, OR 31

You are very warmhearted, but also have a reserved attitude, which can sometimes make you appear unapproachable. If you try to be more outgoing and sociable, you should become more popular. You have a calm and patient manner, and are suited to a career as an academic or a researcher.

DAY 5, 14, OR 23

Your fiery, obstinate nature can sometimes make it difficult for you to accept suggestions or opinions from others, and your stubbornness may lead to quarrels or problems. You should be lucky with money, and may often use your profits to set up new projects. Your innate intelligence will enable you to cope with a demanding career.

DAY 6, 15, OR 24

You have an open, stable, and cheerful character, and enjoy an active social life. You are affectionate and emotional, and have a tendency to daydream. This can lead to confusion, and your eagerness to help others may be stifled by your indecision. Although you will never be wealthy, you should always have enough money.

DAY 7, 16, OR 25

You enjoy a certain amount of excitement in your life, but must learn to become more realistic and disciplined. Although you are a natural performer, you should beware of alienating your friends or colleagues. In your career, the opportunity to travel is more important to you than a good salary or a high standard of living.

DAY 8, 17, OR 26

You have good judgement, but should not act too quickly. Your social skills may sometimes be lacking, and you may alienate other people, so try to be more tactful. You will experience poverty, but also wealth. Your calm and determined nature is combined with a free spirit, making you best suited to self-employment.

DAY 9, 18, OR 27

You are happy, optimistic, and warmhearted. You keep yourself busy, and are rarely troubled by trivialities. Occasionally you quarrel unnecessarily with your friends, and it is important for you to learn to control your moods. You are particularly suited to a career as a sole director or proprietor.

YOUR CHINESE
HOUR OF BIRTH

In Chinese time, one hour is equal to two Western hours.
Each Chinese double hour is associated with one of the
twelve astrological animals.

11 P.M. – 1 A.M. RAT HOUR
You are independent and have a hot temper. Try to think before you speak. Your thrifty nature will be useful in business and at home. You are always willing to help those who are close to you, and they will return your support.

1 – 3 A.M. OX HOUR
Up to the age of twenty, your life could be difficult, but your fortunes are likely to improve after these troublesome years. In your career, be prepared to take a risk or to leave home during your youth to achieve your goals. You should enjoy a prosperous old age.

3 – 5 A.M. TIGER HOUR
You have a lively and creative nature, which may cause family arguments in your youth. Between the ages of twenty and forty you may have many problems. Luckily, your fortunes are likely to improve dramatically in your forties.

5 – 7 A.M. RABBIT HOUR
Your parents should be helpful, but your siblings may be your rivals. You may have to move away from home to achieve your full potential at work. Your committed relationship may take time to become settled, but you should get along much better with everyone after middle age.

7 – 9 A.M. DRAGON HOUR
You have a quick-witted, determined, and attractive nature. Your life will be busy, but you could sometimes be lonely. You should achieve a good standard of living. Try to curb your excessive self-confidence, for it could make working relationships difficult.

9 – 11 A.M. SNAKE HOUR

You have a talent for business and should find it easy to build your career and provide for your family. You have a particularly generous spirit, and will gladly help your friends when they are in trouble. Unfortunately, family relationships are unlikely to run smoothly.

11 A.M. – 1 P.M. HORSE HOUR

You are active, clever, and obstinate. Try to listen to advice. You are fascinated with travel and with changing your life. Learn to control your extravagance, for it could lead to financial suffering.

1 – 3 P.M. RAM HOUR

Steady relationships with your family, friends, or partners are difficult, because you have an active nature. You are clever, but must not force your views on others. Your fortunes are likely to be at their lowest in your middle age.

3 – 5 P.M. MONKEY HOUR

You earn and spend money easily. Your character is attractive, but frustrating, too. Sometimes your parents are not able to give you adequate moral support. Your committed relationship should be good, but do not brood over emotional problems for too long – if you do your career could suffer.

5 – 7 P.M. ROOSTER HOUR

In your teenage years you may have many arguments with your family. There could even be a family division, which should eventually be resolved. You are trustworthy, kind, and warmhearted, and never intend to hurt other people.

7 – 9 P.M. DOG HOUR

Your brave, capable, hard-working nature is ideally suited to self-employment, and the forecast for your career is excellent. Try to control your impatience and vanity. The quality of your life is far more important to you than the amount of money you have saved.

9 – 11 P.M. PIG HOUR

You are particularly skilled at manual work and always set yourself the highest of standards. Although you are warmhearted, you do not like to surround yourself with too many friends. However, the people who are close to you have your complete trust. You can be easily upset by others, but are able to forgive and forget quickly.

YOUR FORTUNE IN OTHER ANIMAL YEARS

The Ox's fortunes fluctuate during the twelve animal years.
It is best to concentrate on a year's positive aspects, and to
take care when faced with the seemingly negative.

YEAR OF THE RAT
This is a year of mixed
fortunes. You are likely to
be prone to illness
throughout the Year of the Rat.
However, do not despair – not
everything is doom and gloom.
Somewhat surprisingly, your career
should progress smoothly this year.

YEAR OF THE OX
It may seem unjust, but
the Year of the Ox is not
necessarily a good year for
an Ox. Your business, or your
career, is likely to come under
considerable threat, and areas in
which you thought you might
succeed could prove disappointing.

YEAR OF THE TIGER
Your family life is
particularly auspicious this
year, and marriage and

children feature highly. Try to
ensure that you spend enough quality
time with your family during this
excellent year.

YEAR OF THE RABBIT
Unfortunately, the Year
of the Rabbit is an
extremely inauspicious
year for the Ox. Nothing will go
smoothly – you are likely to
experience many difficulties, and
illness and even death will seem to
stalk your distant relatives.

YEAR OF THE DRAGON
Although the Year of the
Dragon is a year in which
you feel engulfed by
troubles and problems, do not give
in to feelings of despair. As long as
you manage to keep yourself calm,
you should find that everything can
eventually be resolved.

YEAR OF THE SNAKE

Your fortunes are mixed in the Year of the Snake. For some of the time you will be successful, and money will be abundant. Suddenly, however, you will have to struggle against bad decisions, and will find yourself engaged in disagreements.

YEAR OF THE HORSE

This is a year in which you are well advised to stay calm, keep your own counsel, and bide your time. Try not to rush yourself in any areas of your life. Instead, be content to wait patiently for the benefits that time will inevitably bring.

YEAR OF THE RAM

Try to protect yourself, and beware of people who would like to take advantage of you, or even cheat you. It is important not to let your guard slip, because this year you are susceptible to people who might want to disrupt your life.

YEAR OF THE MONKEY

Success follows you doggedly in the Year of the Monkey – everything that you decide to turn your hand to works out astonishingly well. You will enjoy this year most if you celebrate this seemingly never-ending success with your family.

YEAR OF THE ROOSTER

It may seem unfair, but many of your friends could turn against you. Consequently, you are likely to find the Year of the Rooster very difficult, and your career is likely to suffer as a result.

YEAR OF THE DOG

This is an interesting year. It is likely to be a time of travel, but also of loneliness. There will be many significant changes in your life, and some trouble, too, but the Year of the Dog should also be a time of considerable opportunity.

YEAR OF THE PIG

It is important for you to exercise care and restraint during the Year of the Pig. Your finances are likely to be overstretched, and as a result, you may find yourself having many serious disagreements with members of your family.

YOUR CHINESE
YEAR OF BIRTH

*Your astrological animal corresponds to the Chinese year of
your birth. It is the single most important key in the quest
to unlock your Chinese horoscope.*

Find your Western year of birth in
the left-hand column of the chart.
Your Chinese astrological animal is
on the same line as your year of
birth, in the right-hand column of
the chart. If you were born in the
beginning of the year, check the

middle column of the chart carefully.
For example, if you were born in
1962, you might assume that you
belong to the Year of the Tiger.
However, if your birthday falls
before 5 February, you actually
belong to the Year of the Ox.

1900	31 Jan – 18 Feb 1901	Rat
1901	19 Feb – 7 Feb 1902	Ox
1902	8 Feb – 28 Jan 1903	Tiger
1903	29 Jan – 15 Feb 1904	Rabbit
1904	16 Feb – 3 Feb 1905	Dragon
1905	4 Feb – 24 Jan 1906	Snake
1906	25 Jan – 12 Feb 1907	Horse
1907	13 Feb – 1 Feb 1908	Ram
1908	2 Feb – 21 Jan 1909	Monkey
1909	22 Jan – 9 Feb 1910	Rooster
1910	10 Feb – 29 Jan 1911	Dog
1911	30 Jan – 17 Feb 1912	Pig
1912	18 Feb – 5 Feb 1913	Rat
1913	6 Feb – 25 Jan 1914	Ox
1914	26 Jan – 13 Feb 1915	Tiger
1915	14 Feb – 2 Feb 1916	Rabbit
1916	3 Feb – 22 Jan 1917	Dragon

1917	23 Jan – 10 Feb 1918	Snake
1918	11 Feb – 31 Jan 1919	Horse
1919	1 Feb – 19 Feb 1920	Ram
1920	20 Feb – 7 Feb 1921	Monkey
1921	8 Feb – 27 Jan 1922	Rooster
1922	28 Jan – 15 Feb 1923	Dog
1923	16 Feb – 4 Feb 1924	Pig
1924	5 Feb – 23 Jan 1925	Rat
1925	24 Jan – 12 Feb 1926	Ox
1926	13 Feb – 1 Feb 1927	Tiger
1927	2 Feb – 22 Jan 1928	Rabbit
1928	23 Jan – 9 Feb 1929	Dragon
1929	10 Feb – 29 Jan 1930	Snake
1930	30 Jan – 16 Feb 1931	Horse
1931	17 Feb – 5 Feb 1932	Ram
1932	6 Feb – 25 Jan 1933	Monkey
1933	26 Jan – 13 Feb 1934	Rooster

1934	14 Feb – 3 Feb 1935	Dog	1971	27 Jan – 14 Feb 1972	Pig
1935	4 Feb – 23 Jan 1936	Pig	1972	15 Feb – 2 Feb 1973	Rat
1936	24 Jan – 10 Feb 1937	Rat	1973	3 Feb – 22 Jan 1974	Ox
1937	11 Feb – 30 Jan 1938	Ox	1974	23 Jan – 10 Feb 1975	Tiger
1938	31 Jan – 18 Feb 1939	Tiger	1975	11 Feb – 30 Jan 1976	Rabbit
1939	19 Feb – 7 Feb 1940	Rabbit	1976	31 Jan – 17 Feb 1977	Dragon
1940	8 Feb – 26 Jan 1941	Dragon	1977	18 Feb – 6 Feb 1978	Snake
1941	27 Jan – 14 Feb 1942	Snake	1978	7 Feb – 27 Jan 1979	Horse
1942	15 Feb – 4 Feb 1943	Horse	1979	28 Jan – 15 Feb 1980	Ram
1943	5 Feb – 24 Jan 1944	Ram	1980	16 Feb – 4 Feb 1981	Monkey
1944	25 Jan – 12 Feb 1945	Monkey	1981	5 Feb – 24 Jan 1982	Rooster
1945	13 Feb – 1 Feb 1946	Rooster	1982	25 Jan – 12 Feb 1983	Dog
1946	2 Feb – 21 Jan 1947	Dog	1983	13 Feb – 1 Feb 1984	Pig
1947	22 Jan – 9 Feb 1948	Pig	1984	2 Feb – 19 Feb 1985	Rat
1948	10 Feb – 28 Jan 1949	Rat	1985	20 Feb – 8 Feb 1986	Ox
1949	29 Jan – 16 Feb 1950	Ox	1986	9 Feb – 28 Jan 1987	Tiger
1950	17 Feb – 5 Feb 1951	Tiger	1987	29 Jan – 16 Feb 1988	Rabbit
1951	6 Feb – 26 Jan 1952	Rabbit	1988	17 Feb – 5 Feb 1989	Dragon
1952	27 Jan – 13 Feb 1953	Dragon	1989	6 Feb – 26 Jan 1990	Snake
1953	14 Feb – 2 Feb 1954	Snake	1990	27 Jan – 14 Feb 1991	Horse
1954	3 Feb – 23 Jan 1955	Horse	1991	15 Feb – 3 Feb 1992	Ram
1955	24 Jan – 11 Feb 1956	Ram	1992	4 Feb – 22 Jan 1993	Monkey
1956	12 Feb – 30 Jan 1957	Monkey	1993	23 Jan – 9 Feb 1994	Rooster
1957	31 Jan – 17 Feb 1958	Rooster	1994	10 Feb – 30 Jan 1995	Dog
1958	18 Feb – 7 Feb 1959	Dog	1995	31 Jan – 18 Feb 1996	Pig
1959	8 Feb – 27 Jan 1960	Pig	1996	19 Feb – 6 Feb 1997	Rat
1960	28 Jan – 14 Feb 1961	Rat	1997	7 Feb – 27 Jan 1998	Ox
1961	15 Feb – 4 Feb 1962	Ox	1998	28 Jan – 15 Feb 1999	Tiger
1962	5 Feb – 24 Jan 1963	Tiger	1999	16 Feb – 4 Feb 2000	Rabbit
1963	25 Jan – 12 Feb 1964	Rabbit	2000	5 Feb – 23 Jan 2001	Dragon
1964	13 Feb – 1 Feb 1965	Dragon	2001	24 Jan – 11 Feb 2002	Snake
1965	2 Feb – 20 Jan 1966	Snake	2002	12 Feb – 31 Jan 2003	Horse
1966	21 Jan – 8 Feb 1967	Horse	2003	1 Feb – 21 Jan 2004	Ram
1967	9 Feb – 29 Jan 1968	Ram	2004	22 Jan – 8 Feb 2005	Monkey
1968	30 Jan – 16 Feb 1969	Monkey	2005	9 Feb – 28 Jan 2006	Rooster
1969	17 Feb – 5 Feb 1970	Rooster	2006	29 Jan – 17 Feb 2007	Dog
1970	6 Feb – 26 Jan 1971	Dog	2007	18 Feb – 6 Feb 2008	Pig